The People Factor: Unlocking the Power of Talent in Operations

Daniel Robosky

First Edition published by Daniel Robosky 2023

Copyright © 2023 by Daniel Robosky

All rights reserved. No part of this publication may be reproduced, stored or transmitted in any form or by any means, electronic, mechanical, photocopying, recording, scanning, or otherwise without written permission from the publisher. It is illegal to copy this book, post it to a website, or distribute it by any other means without permission.

Daniel Robosky asserts the moral right to be identified as the author of this work.

First Edition

One

Chapter 1: Introduction – The People Factor in Operations

Welcome to "The People Factor: Unlocking the Power of Talent in Operations." This book is an exploration of the crucial yet often overlooked aspect of operations management—the human component. Our journey is aimed at reevaluating the conventional understanding of operations management and shifting the spotlight onto its most important elements—people.

Operations management has traditionally been a systems and process-driven field. However, these systems and processes do not run on their own. Instead, they are powered by people—individuals who create, operate, manage, and enhance these systems. It is the human element that brings operations to life, an aspect we term as 'The People Factor'. This introduction sets the foundation for understanding why people are instrumental to operational success and why organizations should invest in nurturing this potential.

The Indispensability of Human Touch in Operations

The first concept we'll explore is the irreplaceability of the human touch in operations. Technological advancements have automated many operational aspects, yet there's an integral part of operations where human intuition, creativity, and judgment remain essential.

Imagine a scenario where an unforeseen complication arises in a project. The automated system, programmed to deal with predefined situations, is at a loss, unable to understand or resolve the issue. It's at this juncture that the value of human problem-solving capabilities shines. A member of your team steps in, utilizes their experience, judgment, and creativity, and devises a solution to keep the project on track. Such human interventions are critical to maintaining operational continuity in a dynamic business environment.

Moreover, the ability to understand nuanced customer needs and deliver personalized services is a distinctly human capability. Automated systems can gather data and identify patterns, but it's your workforce that interprets this data, understands its implications, and personalizes the client experience. This human-centric approach is indispensable for driving customer satisfaction and building strong client relationships.

The Driving Force of Innovation

Our second focal point is recognizing people as the drivers of innovation. The business world's competitive nature necessitates continual evolution and improvement. It is the human element within the operations that can propel this growth.

People, with their diverse skills, experiences, and perspectives, are a goldmine of innovation. They see the challenges, inefficiencies, and opportunities within operational processes that automated systems can't perceive. It's their ideas, coupled with their willingness to challenge the status quo, that lead to game-changing improvements and innovations.

For instance, think about a team member who identifies a recurring process bottleneck. They propose an innovative solution that not only resolves the issue but also enhances overall operational efficiency. Such instances underline how the workforce can be the driving force behind process innovation and operational improvement.

The Face and Voice of an Organization

Finally, the workforce forms the organization's face and voice. They embody the organization's values, shape its culture, and interact with clients. A motivated, skilled, and engaged workforce significantly contributes to creating a positive organizational image and nurturing robust client relationships.

Consider the way your employees engage with clients or stakeholders. Their attitude, expertise, and commitment reflect your organization's values, impacting the client's perception of your business. Similarly, an empowering and inclusive culture within the organization, driven by its people, enhances employee engagement and productivity, further strengthening the organization's reputation.

In the chapters that follow, we'll delve into how to recruit the right talent for operations, develop their skills and capabilities, and strategies to empower them. This book synthesizes research findings, industry practices, and real-world case studies to provide a comprehensive understanding and actionable insights into the 'People Factor' in operations.

Our journey is about a transformative shift - recognizing and valuing the architects of operational success—the people. As we navigate this journey together, you will acquire the knowledge and tools to unlock the power

of talent in your operations, driving operational success, and fostering organizational growth.

We invite you to join us in this exploration of "The People Factor: Unlocking the Power of Talent in Operations". Let's unravel the potential of human resources in your operations.

Two

Chapter 2: Harnessing the Military Structure for Operational Success

The Chain of Command

In the military, the chain of command is well-defined and meticulously structured. There is no ambiguity—each person knows precisely who they report to and who reports to them. This hierarchical model ensures that everyone knows their place in the broader scheme of things, enabling streamlined communication and establishing a sense of discipline and accountability.

By introducing such clarity in your business operations, you create an environment of trust and efficiency. It ensures a seamless flow of information, with everyone aware of their role and responsibilities. This transparency can foster better team coordination, enhancing overall productivity and reducing the risk of conflicts or misunderstanding.

Strategic Planning and Execution

Every successful military operation relies heavily on strategic planning and execution. Military leaders spend an extensive amount of time meticulously mapping out their plan of action, forecasting potential scenarios, and assigning resources. This systematic approach ensures preparedness for a variety of situations, leading to a higher probability of success.

Businesses can adopt a similar approach to bolster their operations. Detailed planning—right from understanding the problem, setting objectives, analyzing potential scenarios, devising action plans, and allocating resources—can enable your operations to anticipate potential challenges and devise effective strategies to overcome them. This proactive approach will not only mitigate risks but also ensure optimal utilization of resources and enhance operational efficiency.

Teamwork and Collaboration

Teamwork is not just a concept in the military—it's a matter of survival and mission success. Military personnel are trained to work as a cohesive unit, with each member understanding their role and how it contributes to the larger objective. This sense of camaraderie and interdependence creates a bond that enables the team to overcome adversity together.

In the business context, fostering such a culture of teamwork can significantly impact operational efficiency and employee morale. By promoting collaboration, employees can share knowledge, learn from each other, and work towards common goals. Furthermore, it encourages a sense of belonging, which can significantly enhance employee motivation, engagement, and overall productivity.

Training and Development

The military places a high emphasis on continuous training and development. This rigorous training is designed to equip personnel with the skills required to handle a plethora of scenarios. Such an investment in human capital increases resilience, readiness, and effectiveness.

Similarly, businesses that prioritize continuous training and development of their employees can significantly enhance their operational outcomes. By ensuring that your workforce is equipped with the latest skills and knowledge, you can improve their productivity, enhance job satisfaction, and reduce employee turnover. Additionally, it prepares your team to adapt to the dynamic business environment, allowing your operations to evolve in line with industry trends and technological advancements.

Discipline and Accountability

Discipline and accountability form the bedrock of the military structure. Each person is expected to uphold their responsibilities with utmost diligence and integrity. This culture fosters reliability, improves efficiency, and underpins the success of military operations.

Inculcating such discipline and accountability in business operations can lead to numerous benefits. Employees who understand their responsibilities and the implications of their actions are likely to perform their roles more diligently. It instills a sense of responsibility, leading to improved task completion, better decision-making, and a culture of integrity. This not only boosts operational efficiency but also enhances the organization's reputation.

To summarize, businesses can significantly improve their operations by integrating aspects of the military structure into their operational model. The principles of a clear chain of command, strategic planning and execution, teamwork, continuous training, and accountability can serve as cornerstones for operational efficiency, resilience, and success. By fostering these values, you can unlock the full potential of your workforce, streamline your operations, and set your organization on the path of sustained growth and success.

Three

Chapter 3: The Art of Recruitment: Attracting the Right Talent for Your Operations

Building on the principles of military structure discussed in the previous chapter, this chapter shifts the focus to the first step in harnessing the 'People Factor' in operations: Recruitment. Acquiring the right talent is akin to assembling your army - a task that requires careful planning, precise execution, and an eye for potential.

Understanding the Role Requirements

The first stage of the recruitment process involves gaining a clear understanding of the role requirements. What are the responsibilities associated with the position? What skills and qualifications are needed? What is the growth trajectory for someone in this role? Understanding the answers to these questions is crucial to define the 'ideal candidate' and ensure that your recruitment efforts are targeted and effective.

In the military, this process of understanding the role requirements is meticulous. Each role, from an infantry soldier to a technical specialist, has a clear set of requirements. By defining these requirements, the military ensures that their recruitment efforts are precise and effective.

Applying this approach to your operations, understanding the role requirements can greatly enhance the efficiency of your recruitment process. It enables you to design precise job descriptions, ask the right questions during interviews, and identify the most suitable candidates for the role. It also helps candidates understand if they're a good fit for the position, thereby attracting those who align with the role requirements and the organization's culture.

Building an Attractive Employer Brand

In today's competitive job market, attracting the right talent requires more than just a job posting. It requires an attractive employer brand - a reputation that your

Chapter 3: The Art of Recruitment: Attracting the Right Talent for Your Operations

organization is a great place to work. An attractive employer brand can help draw high-potential candidates towards your organization and make them eager to be a part of your team.

In the context of the military, patriotism, discipline, the opportunity to serve the nation, and the promise of personal and professional growth all contribute to their strong brand appeal. As a business, it's important to understand what your organization stands for and how to communicate it effectively to potential candidates.

Your employer brand could be built around aspects like positive work culture, opportunities for learning and growth, corporate social responsibility initiatives, or innovative work practices. By consistently communicating and demonstrating these values, you can build an employer brand that resonates with potential candidates and draws them towards your organization.

The Recruitment Process

The recruitment process is the bridge between your organization and potential candidates. It's the medium through which you communicate the job role, assess candidates, and ultimately select the ones best suited for your operations. An effective recruitment process is objective, comprehensive, and efficient.

Drawing from the military recruitment process, which is stringent, rigorous, and designed to test a range of skills, businesses can learn the value of a comprehensive assessment. While academic qualifications and work experience are important, they are not the sole determinants of a candidate's potential. It's essential to assess other aspects like problem-solving skills, adaptability, teamwork, and cultural fit.

By adopting a holistic approach to assessment, you can identify candidates who not only have the right skills but also align with your organization's values and culture. This can greatly enhance the effectiveness of your recruitment process and improve the quality of your hires.

Onboarding and Integration

The final stage of the recruitment process is onboarding and integration. Once you have selected the right candidates, it's crucial to ensure they are properly introduced to the organization, understand their roles and responsibilities, and feel part of the team.

Chapter 3: The Art of Recruitment: Attracting the Right Talent for Your Operations

The military excels in this aspect, with rigorous training programs designed to transform recruits into capable soldiers. For businesses, while the approach may be less intense, the principle remains the same. Effective onboarding helps new hires understand the organization's culture, familiarize themselves with their roles, and start contributing to the operations quickly.

It also helps in building a sense of belonging and commitment, which can greatly enhance job satisfaction and employee retention.

In conclusion, the art of recruitment plays a crucial role in harnessing the power of talent in your operations. By understanding the role requirements, building an attractive employer brand, implementing an effective recruitment process, and ensuring proper onboarding, you can attract, select, and retain the right talent for your operations. These steps set the foundation for a strong and capable workforce that can drive your operations towards success.

Four

Chapter 4: Employee Development: Nurturing Your Operational Workforce

In the wake of assembling a proficient workforce, the focus now shifts towards nurturing the recruited talent. Like a commanding officer who ensures the continual growth and readiness of their troops, your role extends to cultivating an environment conducive to the development and progression of your workforce. This chapter will delve into the importance of employee development, its key elements, and how it ties in with operational success.

Understanding the Importance of Employee Development

Employee development is an integral part of human resource management. It's an ongoing process aimed at improving employees' skills, knowledge, and performance, preparing them for future challenges and career progression. It's a dual-edged sword, providing benefits to both employees and the organization.

For employees, development programs offer opportunities to learn new skills, stay updated with industry trends, and enhance their job performance. They provide a clear path for career progression, boosting employee morale, job satisfaction, and retention.

For organizations, employee development programs lead to a more skilled and competent workforce. They help businesses adapt to changes in the industry and maintain a competitive edge. As employees become more competent, operational efficiency improves, leading to increased productivity and profitability.

The Military's Approach to Training and Development

The military's approach to training and development is comprehensive and continuous. Training starts from the moment a recruit joins and continues throughout their military career. The military understands that their operational success depends heavily on the readiness and competence of their personnel, and they invest significantly in training and development.

The emphasis is not just on hard skills but also on soft skills like leadership, teamwork, communication, and resilience. This holistic approach ensures that personnel are equipped with all the skills they need to perform their roles effectively and adapt to any situation.

Employee Development Strategies for Businesses

Drawing insights from the military's approach, businesses can implement several strategies for effective employee development:

1. On-the-Job Training: This is one of the most effective methods of training. It involves employees learning skills while performing their roles. On-the-job training could involve job shadowing, coaching, or rotational assignments. It allows employees to learn by doing, providing a practical understanding of the job.

2. Off-the-Job Training: This refers to training programs conducted outside the regular work environment. These could include seminars, workshops, courses, or conferences. Off-the-job training provides employees with a break from the daily routine, offering an opportunity to learn new skills and knowledge.

3. E-Learning: With the advancement of technology, e-learning has become a popular method for employee development. It provides flexibility, allowing employees to learn at their own pace. It can also be cost-effective and easily scalable across the organization.

4. Leadership Development: Developing the leadership skills of your employees is critical for operational success. It helps in identifying and nurturing future leaders within the organization. Leadership development programs could include mentoring, leadership courses, or experiential learning.

5. Feedback and Performance Reviews: Regular feedback and performance reviews are vital for employee development. They provide employees with an understanding of their strengths and areas for improvement. Feedback should be constructive, actionable, and aimed at helping the employee improve their performance.

6. Career Development Planning: This involves creating a roadmap for each employee's career progression within the organization. Career development plans should be personalized, taking into account the employee's aspirations, skills, and potential. They provide employees

with a clear path for advancement, enhancing job satisfaction and retention.

7. Continual Learning: Encouraging a culture of continual learning can foster a highly skilled and adaptable workforce. This could involve providing access to online courses, industry literature, or skill development programs.

In conclusion, employee development is a crucial component in unlocking the power of talent in operations. By investing in your workforce's development, you can create a team that is competent, motivated, and prepared for the dynamic business environment. This not only enhances operational efficiency but also paves the way for sustained organizational growth and success.ment: Nurturing Your Operational Workforce.

Five

Chapter 5: The Power of Employee Engagement: Driving Operational Excellence

Continuing our journey in harnessing the 'People Factor' in operations, this chapter examines the pivotal role of employee engagement. Much like a well-drilled military unit, an engaged workforce can drive operational excellence, create a positive work environment, and contribute significantly to an organization's success. We'll delve into understanding employee engagement, its benefits, and strategies to promote it within your organization.

Understanding Employee Engagement

Employee engagement is a measure of an employee's emotional commitment and dedication to their organization and its goals. It's about more than just job satisfaction; an engaged employee feels a deep connection with the organization, goes the extra mile, and takes personal pride in their work.

Benefits of Employee Engagement

The benefits of having an engaged workforce are manifold. It impacts almost every aspect of operations, providing both tangible and intangible benefits.

1. **Productivity**: Engaged employees are often more productive. Their commitment and enthusiasm towards their work lead to higher performance levels. They are motivated to deliver their best, driving operational efficiency.

2. **Retention:** High levels of engagement contribute to lower turnover rates. When employees are engaged, they are more likely to remain with the organization, reducing the cost and disruption of employee turnover.

3. **Innovation**: Engaged employees tend to be more innovative. They are more likely to contribute ideas,

participate in problem-solving, and drive innovation in operations.

4. **Customer Satisfaction**: Engaged employees often provide better customer service. They are committed to the organization's success, which is directly linked to customer satisfaction.

5. **Profitability**: All the above benefits, including increased productivity, innovation, and customer satisfaction, contribute to increased profitability. A highly engaged workforce is a valuable asset that can drive business success.

Building an Employee Engagement Strategy

Building an effective employee engagement strategy requires a comprehensive approach. Here are some strategies to consider:

1. **Clear Communication**: Clear and open communication is the foundation of employee engagement. Employees should be aware of the organization's mission, goals, and strategies. Regular updates and an open-door policy can foster transparency and trust.

2. **Recognition and Rewards**: Recognizing and rewarding employees for their efforts can boost morale and engagement. It shows employees that their contributions are valued, encouraging them to continue delivering their best.

3. **Work Environment:** A positive work environment is crucial for engagement. This includes physical aspects, like a safe and comfortable workspace, as well as psychological aspects, like a culture of respect and collaboration.

4. **Employee Development****: As discussed in the previous chapter, employee development is crucial for engagement. Employees who see a clear path for growth and development within the organization are more likely to be engaged.

5. **Leadership**: Effective leadership plays a critical role in driving employee engagement. Leaders who are approachable, supportive, and inspire confidence can significantly boost engagement levels.

6. **Work-Life Balance**: Supporting work-life balance is another important factor. Flexible work hours, remote working options, and adequate leave policies can contribute to higher engagement.

7. **Employee Surveys**: Regular employee surveys can help gauge engagement levels and identify areas for improvement. They provide valuable insights into employees' experiences and perceptions.

8. **Community Involvement**: Encouraging employees to participate in community activities can foster a sense of purpose and belonging, enhancing engagement.

In conclusion, promoting employee engagement is critical for operational excellence. An engaged workforce is more productive, innovative, and committed to the organization's success. By implementing a comprehensive employee engagement strategy, you can harness the full potential of your workforce, enhancing operational efficiency, and driving sustained business growth.

Six

Chapter 6: Building a High-Performing Team: The Key to Operational Success

Building a high-performing team is an essential aspect of driving operational success. It's not merely about gathering a group of talented individuals; it requires creating an environment where everyone works towards a common goal, understands their roles, communicates effectively, and feels valued. In this chapter, we'll delve into the steps involved in building a high-performing team and the strategies that can be employed to maintain its momentum.

Understanding High-Performing Teams

A high-performing team can be described as a group of individuals with complementary skills who share a common vision, are driven by performance goals, and work interdependently towards achieving these goals. Such teams exhibit high levels of collaboration, creativity, and productivity, and significantly contribute to operational success.

The Characteristics of High-Performing Teams

High-performing teams possess certain key characteristics. Understanding these attributes can serve as a guide when building and nurturing your team:

1. Clear Purpose and Goals: High-performing teams are aligned with the organization's vision and have well-defined, measurable goals. They understand the bigger picture and their role in achieving it.

2. Complementary Skills: These teams comprise members with diverse but complementary skills. This diversity enriches the team, allowing them to approach problems from different perspectives and come up with creative solutions.

3. Effective Communication: High levels of transparency and effective communication are hallmarks of high-performing teams. They foster an environment where ideas, feedback, and challenges can be freely discussed.

4. Mutual Accountability: Members of high-performing teams take ownership of their tasks and feel a shared sense of responsibility towards team goals.

5. Strong Leadership: Effective team leaders play a crucial role in guiding the team, resolving conflicts, and ensuring everyone stays motivated and focused on the goals.

Steps to Building a High-Performing Team

Building a high-performing team is a process that requires strategic planning, careful execution, and ongoing management. Here are the key steps involved in this process:

1. Define the Purpose and Goals: Start by clearly defining the team's purpose and what it aims to achieve. Make sure these align with the overall organizational goals. Clearly articulated goals serve as a roadmap for the team's efforts.

2. Assemble the Team: When selecting team members, consider their skills, experiences, and working styles. Look for a mix of skills that complement each other. The right team composition can greatly enhance the team's performance.

3. Establish Roles and Responsibilities: Once the team is formed, clarify each member's role and responsibilities. This helps avoid confusion, overlaps, and gaps in work, ensuring that all areas of operation are covered.

4. Foster a Collaborative Culture: Encourage a culture of collaboration where ideas and knowledge are freely shared. This promotes collective problem-solving and decision-making, enhancing the team's effectiveness.

5. Implement Effective Communication Channels: Implement communication channels that facilitate easy and transparent communication among team members. Regular team meetings, project management tools, and virtual communication platforms can be very effective.

6. Provide Necessary Training: Equip your team with the necessary skills and knowledge to perform their roles effectively. This could involve technical training, soft skills development, or team-building activities.

7. Set Performance Metrics: Establish clear performance metrics to measure the team's progress towards its goals. Regularly review these metrics and provide constructive feedback to help the team improve.

8. Recognize and Reward Performance: Recognizing and rewarding team and individual performances can boost morale and motivation. Celebrate successes, no matter how small, and appreciate team members for their contributions.

Maintaining a High-Performing Team

Building a high-performing team is just the first step. Maintaining its performance over time requires ongoing effort. Here are some strategies to consider:

1. Regular Team Building: Regular team-building activities can help strengthen bonds, improve communication, and resolve any interpersonal issues. These activities can range from simple ice-breaking sessions to complex problem-solving exercises.

2. Encourage Continuous Learning: Foster a culture of continuous learning within the team. Encourage members to upgrade their skills and stay updated with industry trends. Provide learning resources and opportunities for professional development.

3. Manage Conflict: Conflict is inevitable in any team. However, it's important to manage it effectively to prevent it from affecting team performance. Encourage

open discussion and use conflicts as opportunities for learning and growth.

4. Adapt to Change: High-performing teams are adaptable. They are able to adjust to changes in the environment, tasks, or team structure. Encourage flexibility and resilience among team members.

5. Maintain Work-Life Balance: Ensure that team members are not overworked and have a healthy work-life balance. Overworking can lead to burnout and affect performance. Respect personal time and encourage regular breaks.

In conclusion, building and maintaining a high-performing team is a complex but rewarding process. It requires a strategic approach, effective leadership, and continuous effort. A high-performing team can significantly enhance operational efficiency, drive innovation, and contribute to the overall success of the organization. As such, investing in your team's performance is an investment in your organization's future.

Seven

Chapter 7: Setting Goals and Tracking Team Performance

Goal setting and performance tracking are indispensable components of managing a high-performing team. They provide direction, motivate team members, and offer a clear metric for success. By setting meaningful goals and regularly tracking performance against these goals, teams can optimize their productivity, identify areas for improvement, and drive operational success. In this chapter, we'll delve into effective methods for setting and tracking team goals.

Understanding Goal Setting

Goal setting is the process of defining what a team needs to accomplish and creating a plan to achieve those results. Effective goals should be SMART: Specific, Measurable, Achievable, Relevant, and Time-bound. By setting SMART goals, teams can focus their efforts, align their tasks with the broader organizational objectives, and monitor their progress effectively.

Benefits of Goal Setting

Goal setting has multiple benefits:

1. Provides Direction: Goals serve as a roadmap, guiding team members towards what they need to achieve. They help team members understand what is expected of them, keeping everyone focused and aligned.

2. Enhances Motivation: When goals are clear and achievable, they can boost team members' motivation. Reaching a goal gives a sense of accomplishment, which can fuel motivation and engagement.

3. Facilitates Planning: By knowing what needs to be accomplished, teams can plan their tasks more effectively. They can prioritize activities, allocate resources appropriately, and create timelines for task completion.

4. Improves Decision Making: Goals provide a framework for decision making. They help in determining which decisions align with the goal and which don't.

5. Enhances Performance: Research has shown that setting specific and challenging goals can enhance team performance. They provide a benchmark against which team performance can be measured.

Steps for Effective Goal Setting

Setting effective team goals involves the following steps:

1. Align Goals with Organizational Objectives: The team's goals should align with the broader organizational objectives. This ensures that the team's efforts contribute to the overall success of the organization.

2. Involve Team Members in Goal Setting: Including team members in the goal-setting process can enhance their commitment to the goals. It can also provide valuable insights that can improve the quality of the goals.

3. Make Goals SMART: As mentioned earlier, effective goals are SMART. They should be clear, measurable, achievable, relevant, and time-bound.

4. Break Down Goals into Tasks: Once the goals are set, break them down into smaller tasks. This makes the goals more manageable and allows for easier tracking of progress.

5. Communicate Goals Clearly: Ensure that all team members understand the goals. Clear communication is crucial to avoid misunderstandings and ensure everyone is on the same page.

6. Review and Adjust Goals Regularly: Goals are not set in stone. They should be reviewed regularly and adjusted as needed based on changes in the team's environment or the organization's objectives.

Understanding Performance Tracking

Performance tracking is the process of monitoring and assessing a team's performance against its goals. Regular performance tracking allows teams to understand whether they're on track to achieve their goals, identify areas where they're struggling, and take corrective action.

Benefits of Performance Tracking

Performance tracking provides several benefits:

1. Monitors Progress: Performance tracking allows teams to monitor their progress towards their goals. This helps them understand whether they're on track and what adjustments need to be made.

2. Identifies Issues: Regular performance tracking can help identify issues early. This allows for timely intervention and resolution of problems.

3. Enhances Accountability: Performance tracking enhances accountability within the team. It provides a clear metric against which individual and team performance can be measured.

4. Provides Feedback: Performance tracking provides valuable feedback to team members. It allows them to understand their strengths and areas for improvement.

5. Supports Decision Making: Performance data can support decision making by providing evidence-based insights.

Steps for Effective Performance Tracking

Here are the key steps to effectively track team performance:

1. Define Performance Metrics: Start by defining clear performance metrics that align with the team's goals. These could include productivity metrics, quality metrics, time-based metrics, or any other relevant measures.

2. Set Up a Performance Tracking System: Implement a system to track these metrics. This could be a software tool or a manual system, depending on the team's needs and resources.

3. Monitor Performance Regularly: Regularly monitor performance against these metrics. This will allow you to quickly identify and address any issues.

4. Analyze Performance Data: Don't just collect performance data - analyze it. Look for trends, identify patterns, and draw insights.

5. Provide Constructive Feedback: Use the performance data to provide constructive feedback to team members. Recognize good performance and provide support for improvement where needed.

6. Make Data-Driven Decisions: Use the insights from performance data to make informed decisions. This could involve adjusting goals, changing strategies, or providing additional resources.

In conclusion, setting effective goals and regularly tracking team performance are critical for driving operational success. They provide direction, motivate team members, and provide a framework for decision making. By mastering these processes, teams can optimize their performance and contribute significantly to the organization's success. As such, goal setting and performance tracking should be integral components of every team's operational strategy.

Eight

Chapter 8: The Power and Pitfalls of High-Performing Managers

High-performing managers are vital to any organization's success. They drive team performance, foster innovation, and contribute significantly to operational efficiency. However, if not properly nurtured and guided, these talented individuals can inadvertently become a detriment to the organization. This chapter explores the power of high-performing managers, the potential pitfalls they may encounter, and how organizations can ensure these managers mature effectively to maximize their potential.

Understanding High-Performing Managers

High-performing managers are individuals who consistently excel in their roles. They demonstrate strong leadership skills, achieve outstanding results, and inspire their teams to perform at their best. They exhibit traits like strategic thinking, problem-solving, excellent communication, and emotional intelligence.

The Power of High-Performing Managers

High-performing managers can significantly contribute to an organization's success. Their benefits are manifold:

1. Driving Team Performance: High-performing managers effectively lead their teams to achieve goals. They inspire and motivate their team members, creating an environment conducive to high performance.

2. Fostering Innovation: They encourage creativity and innovation within their teams, driving new ideas, solutions, and improvements in processes and products.

3. Ensuring Operational Efficiency: By strategically managing resources and workflows, these managers ensure efficient operations and high-quality outcomes.

4. Building Organizational Culture: High-performing managers play a crucial role in building and maintaining a positive organizational culture. They set the tone for their

team's behavior, which can significantly influence the overall work environment.

5. Developing Talent: They also focus on developing their team members' skills and capabilities, contributing to the organization's talent pool and succession planning.

Potential Pitfalls and the Need for Managerial Maturity

Despite their exceptional performance, high-performing managers can encounter potential pitfalls. If not addressed properly, these can be detrimental to both the manager and the organization.

1. Overconfidence: Success can sometimes lead to overconfidence, making managers resistant to feedback and less likely to recognize their areas for improvement.

2. Burnout: High-performing managers often have high levels of commitment and can push themselves to the point of burnout, affecting their health and performance.

3. Neglecting Team Development: Focused on achieving results, they may neglect the development needs of their team members.

4. Micromanagement: They may feel the need to control all aspects of their team's work, which can stifle team members' autonomy and creativity.

5. Resistance to Delegation: Given their capability and drive to deliver high-quality results, they may resist delegating tasks, creating a bottleneck in the team's operations.

To prevent these pitfalls, it's essential for organizations to help high-performing managers mature effectively. This involves providing them with the right support and guidance to hone their leadership skills, balance their workload, and navigate their career progression.

Developing and Supporting High-Performing Managers

Organizations can take several steps to support the development and maturity of their high-performing managers:

1. Provide Continuous Learning Opportunities: High-performing managers, like any professionals, need to continually update and expand their skills. Providing them with learning opportunities can help them improve

their managerial capabilities and adapt to changing circumstances.

2. Foster a Feedback Culture: Encourage a culture of regular, constructive feedback. This can help managers recognize their strengths and areas for improvement and foster a growth mindset.

3. Prioritize Wellbeing: Organizations need to acknowledge the risk of burnout among high-performing managers and take steps to promote their wellbeing. This could include encouraging work-life balance, providing mental health resources, and promoting resilience.

4. Encourage Delegation and Empowerment: Teach high-performing managers the importance and techniques of effective delegation. Encourage them to empower their team members by giving them autonomy and decision-making authority.

5. Provide Mentorship and Coaching: Mentorship and coaching can provide managers with guidance and insights from more experienced colleagues. This can help them navigate their career path, make informed decisions, and avoid common pitfalls.

In conclusion, high-performing managers have the potential to drive significant benefits for organizations. However, without the right support and guidance, they may encounter pitfalls that could undermine their performance and impact the organization. By providing high-performing managers with the right development opportunities and support, organizations can ensure these managers mature effectively and continue to contribute significantly to their success. It is an investment worth making as the payoff can be immense in terms of enhanced team performance, innovation, and operational efficiency.

Nine

Chapter 9: Fostering Growth and Sustaining High Performance

As we have journeyed through the realm of high-performing teams and managers, we've unearthed the power they hold and the challenges they might encounter. But how does an organization foster their growth and ensure sustained high performance? The ninth chapter of our exploration unfolds the strategies and tactics that organizations can adopt to nurture their high-performing teams and managers and maintain their exceptional performance over time.

Nurturing High-Performing Teams

Sustained high performance from teams doesn't occur by accident. It is the product of deliberate strategies, supportive environments, and continuous learning. Here are some tactics to foster the growth of high-performing teams:

1. Provide Continuous Learning Opportunities: Equip your teams with the skills and knowledge they need to keep up with changes in their industry. Encourage lifelong learning and provide the necessary resources to facilitate it.

2. Develop Leadership within the Team: Every team member has the potential to be a leader in their area. Nurture these leadership skills and provide opportunities for members to step up and lead.

3. Foster Open Communication: Encourage team members to share their thoughts, ideas, and concerns. Open communication builds trust and ensures that everyone is aligned.

4. Recognize and Reward Performance: Acknowledging the hard work and achievements of your team can boost morale and motivation. Recognize and reward individuals and the team as a whole to encourage ongoing high performance.

5. Promote Work-Life Balance: High performance doesn't mean working all the time. Encourage your team to take

care of their physical and mental health, which is crucial for sustained performance.

6. Regularly Review and Update Goals: The business landscape is dynamic. Ensure that the team's goals are always relevant by reviewing and updating them as necessary.

Developing High-Performing Managers

High-performing managers are the backbone of high-performing teams. It is, therefore, vital to invest in their development. Here are strategies to nurture your high-performing managers:

1. Provide Leadership Training: Leadership skills can be developed and honed with proper training. Invest in your managers' growth by providing them with the training they need to lead effectively.

2. Create a Succession Plan: High-performing managers should have a clear career progression path. A succession plan not only motivates the managers but also ensures the organization is prepared for the future.

3. Encourage Networking: Connections and collaborations can provide managers with new perspectives and insights.

Encourage them to network both within and outside the organization.

4. Provide Mentorship: Pair your managers with experienced mentors who can guide them, challenge them, and provide feedback.

5. Foster Resilience: Resilience is a critical skill for high-performing managers. Provide them with the resources and support they need to bounce back from setbacks.

Maintaining High Performance

Maintaining high performance involves a cycle of setting goals, measuring performance, giving feedback, and continuous learning. Here's how to keep the cycle moving:

1. Monitor Performance: Regularly track your teams' and managers' performance against their goals. Use the data to identify areas of strength and areas that need improvement.

2. Provide Regular Feedback: Timely, constructive feedback helps teams and managers understand how they're doing and what they need to improve. Make

feedback a regular part of your performance management process.

3. Encourage Self-Assessment: Empower your teams and managers by encouraging them to assess their own performance. Self-assessment can lead to self-awareness, which is key to personal growth and development.

4. Update Goals and Strategies: As your organization evolves, so should your goals and strategies. Regularly review and update them to ensure they stay relevant.

5. Foster a Growth Mindset: Encourage a mindset that sees challenges as opportunities for growth. A growth mindset can fuel continuous learning and improvement.

Fostering growth and sustaining high performance in teams and managers is a dynamic, ongoing process. It requires a concerted effort from the entire organization - from top leadership to individual team members. By investing in their development, providing regular feedback, and maintaining a focus on continuous learning, organizations can cultivate a high-performance culture that delivers lasting success.

Ten

Chapter 10: Maintaining Momentum and Identifying Promotion Opportunities

After fostering the growth of high-performing teams and managers, the challenge for organizations is to maintain the momentum and ensure their sustained success. This involves not just consistently nurturing their skills and capabilities, but also recognizing when it's the right time to promote these high performers. This chapter delves into strategies for maintaining performance momentum and accurately identifying promotion opportunities.

Maintaining Performance Momentum

Maintaining momentum requires a delicate balance of pushing for continued growth while also recognizing and

Chapter 10: Maintaining Momentum and Identifying Promotion Opportunities

celebrating current successes. Below are some strategies to maintain performance momentum:

1. Establish Clear and Evolving Goals: Ensure your teams and managers always have clear goals to aim for. These goals should be ambitious but attainable, and they should evolve as your organization grows and changes.

2. Foster a Culture of Continuous Learning: Encourage a culture where ongoing learning and skill development is valued. Provide opportunities for teams and managers to expand their knowledge and expertise through trainings, workshops, conferences, and other learning initiatives.

3. Recognize and Reward Success: Regular recognition of success can motivate your teams and managers to continue performing at a high level. This could be through verbal acknowledgement, awards, bonuses, or other forms of recognition that resonate within your organization.

4. Encourage Innovation: High performers are often driven by the opportunity to innovate and make a significant impact. Encourage innovative thinking and provide the necessary resources for teams and managers to implement new ideas.

5. Promote Collaboration: High performance doesn't occur in a vacuum. Encourage collaboration between teams and managers to share knowledge, tackle challenges, and drive collective success.

Identifying Promotion Opportunities

Promoting high performers at the right time is crucial. It not only rewards them for their hard work, but also positions them to make an even greater impact within the organization. However, it's crucial to promote high performers when they are ready, both in terms of skills and mindset. Here are some strategies to accurately identify promotion opportunities:

1. Assess Readiness: Before promoting high performers, assess their readiness for a higher role. This involves evaluating their technical skills, leadership abilities, strategic thinking, and emotional intelligence. Tools such as 360-degree feedback can provide a comprehensive view of an individual's capabilities.

2. Look Beyond Performance: While performance is a significant factor, it shouldn't be the only consideration. Look at the individual's potential to grow, their ability to inspire others, their strategic thinking capabilities, and their alignment with the organization's values and culture.

3. Consider Aspirations: Understand the career aspirations of your high performers. Promotion should align with their career goals and their personal vision of success.

4. Monitor Performance Over Time: Consistency is key when considering promotions. Monitor the individual's performance over time to ensure they consistently deliver results and show growth.

5. Involve Mentors and Coaches: Mentors and coaches can provide valuable insights into an individual's readiness for promotion. They can assess not only their performance but also their potential and readiness for a higher role.

Setting Up for Success: Building Growth Criteria

Promotion of high performers is not the end of the journey but rather the start of a new chapter in their professional development. To ensure their continued success, it is important to build a criteria for growth that aligns with their new responsibilities and future career aspirations. Here are some strategies to develop such a criteria:

   1. Define Clear Expectations: As high performers move into higher roles, clarify what is expected from them

in terms of duties, performance standards, and leadership responsibilities. Defining clear expectations can help them understand their new role and direct their efforts effectively.

2. Develop Individual Development Plans: Work with high performers to create individual development plans that outline the skills and knowledge they need to acquire in their new roles. This not only provides a roadmap for their development but also demonstrates your investment in their growth.

3. Provide Leadership Training: As high performers transition into roles with more leadership responsibilities, ensure they are equipped with the necessary leadership skills. This can include strategic decision-making, people management, emotional intelligence, and more.

4. Foster Mentorship: Continue to provide mentorship opportunities as high performers move up the ladder. Mentors who have experience in similar roles can provide valuable guidance and advice.

5. Encourage Networking: As high performers ascend into higher roles, the importance of a strong professional network increases. Encourage them to

Chapter 10: Maintaining Momentum and Identifying Promotion Opportunities

network with peers, industry professionals, and other leaders within the organization.

6. Facilitate Cross-Functional Exposure: To prepare high performers for higher roles, especially those that involve overseeing multiple functions, provide them with opportunities to gain exposure to various parts of the organization.

7. Review and Adjust the Criteria: As high performers grow in their roles and the business environment changes, the criteria for growth may need to be reviewed and adjusted. This ensures that the criteria remains relevant and continues to drive growth in the right direction.

By creating a robust growth criteria for high performers, organizations can better support these individuals as they take on more responsibilities. This approach ensures that promotions are not just a reward for past performance but also a stepping stone for future growth and success.

In conclusion, maintaining performance momentum and identifying promotion opportunities are just the initial steps. Ensuring the continued growth and success of high performers as they transition into higher roles requires thoughtful planning, ongoing support, and a carefully crafted growth criteria. It is this forward-looking and people-centric approach that can truly unlock the power of talent in operations, leading to sustained high performance and long-term organizational success.

Eleven

Chapter 11: Nurturing a Culture of Continuous Improvement

A culture of continuous improvement is a hallmark of high-performing organizations. It is an environment where individuals are encouraged to seek better ways of doing things, learn from mistakes, and embrace innovation. In this chapter, we will explore the importance of nurturing a culture of continuous improvement within operations, the key elements of such a culture, and strategies for fostering it.

The Importance of a Culture of Continuous Improvement

A culture of continuous improvement is vital for organizations to stay competitive and adapt to evolving business landscapes. Here are some reasons why it is crucial:

1. Enhances Operational Efficiency: Continuous improvement initiatives focus on eliminating waste, streamlining processes, and improving efficiency. This leads to cost savings, shorter cycle times, and enhanced productivity.

2. Drives Innovation: A culture that encourages continuous improvement fosters a mindset of innovation. It encourages employees to think outside the box, explore new ideas, and challenge the status quo, resulting in breakthrough innovations.

3. Promotes Employee Engagement: When employees are actively involved in identifying improvement opportunities, they feel valued and empowered. This leads to increased engagement and a sense of ownership in the organization's success.

4. Enhances Customer Satisfaction: Continuous improvement initiatives focus on meeting and exceeding customer expectations. By consistently seeking ways to improve products, services, and processes, organizations can deliver superior customer experiences.

5. Ensures Organizational Agility: In a rapidly changing business environment, organizations need to be agile. A culture of continuous improvement promotes flexibility and adaptability, allowing organizations to respond quickly to market shifts and emerging trends.

Elements of a Culture of Continuous Improvement

Creating a culture of continuous improvement involves cultivating specific elements within the organization. These elements include:

1. Leadership Support: Leaders play a critical role in fostering a culture of continuous improvement. They need to champion the concept, actively participate in improvement initiatives, and provide the necessary resources and support.

2. Employee Empowerment: Employees should feel empowered to identify and address improvement opportunities. They should be encouraged to share their ideas, take ownership of improvement projects, and contribute to the organization's growth.

3. Open Communication: Transparent and open communication channels are essential for sharing improvement ideas, progress updates, and lessons learned.

This encourages collaboration and the exchange of knowledge throughout the organization.

4. Learning and Development: Continuous improvement requires a commitment to ongoing learning and development. Providing training programs, workshops, and resources that enhance employees' problem-solving and critical thinking skills is crucial.

5. Data-Driven Decision Making: Making decisions based on data and metrics is a fundamental aspect of continuous improvement. Organizations need to collect and analyze relevant data to identify improvement opportunities and measure the impact of implemented changes.

Strategies for Fostering a Culture of Continuous Improvement

To nurture a culture of continuous improvement, organizations can adopt the following strategies:

1. Set Clear Expectations: Clearly communicate the organization's commitment to continuous improvement and its importance. Set clear expectations for employees at all levels to actively participate in improvement initiatives.

Chapter 11: Nurturing a Culture of Continuous Improvement

2. Foster Collaboration and Cross-Functional Teams: Create opportunities for employees from different departments or teams to collaborate on improvement projects. This fosters a culture of shared learning and diverse perspectives.

3. Establish Improvement Frameworks: Implement improvement frameworks such as Lean Six Sigma or Kaizen that provide structured approaches to problem-solving and process improvement.

4. Encourage Experimentation and Risk-Taking: Create a safe environment where employees feel comfortable taking risks, experimenting with new ideas, and learning from failures.

5. Recognize and Reward Improvement Efforts: Acknowledge and reward employees' contributions to continuous improvement. This can be done through formal recognition programs, incentives, or public appreciation of achievements.

6. Provide Resources and Support: Ensure that employees have access to the necessary resources, tools, and training to support their

improvement efforts. This may include providing data analysis tools, process improvement methodologies, or specialized training programs.

7. Foster a Learning Culture: Promote a culture of learning and curiosity by encouraging employees to seek out new knowledge, attend conferences or workshops, and share their learnings with others.

8. Continuously Evaluate and Adjust: Regularly evaluate the effectiveness of improvement initiatives and make necessary adjustments based on feedback and results. This iterative approach ensures continuous growth and refinement.

In conclusion, nurturing a culture of continuous improvement is crucial for organizations seeking long-term success. By fostering leadership support, empowering employees, promoting open communication, and implementing strategies to drive improvement, organizations can create an environment where continuous learning, innovation, and efficiency thrive. Embracing a culture of continuous improvement enables organizations to adapt to changing business landscapes, exceed customer expectations, and maintain their competitive edge.

Twelve

Chapter 12: The Power of Talent in Operations: A Journey of Success

As we come to the final chapter of our exploration into the power of talent in operations, it is important to reflect on the transformative journey we have embarked upon. Throughout this book, we have delved into the critical aspects of recruiting, developing, and empowering a skilled operations workforce. We have explored the dynamics of high-performing teams, the role of exceptional managers, the significance of continuous improvement, and the strategies to maintain momentum and foster growth. Now, let us bring it all together and celebrate the power of talent in operations as a catalyst for organizational success.

Recognizing the Impact of Talent in Operations

Talent is the lifeblood of any organization. In the realm of operations, it is the people who drive efficiency, innovation, and excellence. They are the ones who optimize processes, optimize supply chains, and deliver exceptional customer experiences. By recognizing and harnessing the power of talent, organizations can unlock their full potential and achieve remarkable success.

Creating a Culture of Talent Excellence

Building a culture of talent excellence is the foundation for leveraging the power of talent in operations. It requires a holistic approach that encompasses every aspect of talent management, from recruitment to retention. Here are key strategies to foster a culture of talent excellence:

1. Strategic Workforce Planning: Align talent strategies with the organization's strategic objectives. Anticipate future talent needs, identify skill gaps, and develop plans to attract and develop the right talent.

2. Robust Recruitment and Selection Processes: Implement rigorous recruitment and selection processes to ensure the right individuals are brought into the organization. This includes defining clear job profiles,

conducting thorough assessments, and considering cultural fit.

3. Continuous Development and Learning: Provide ongoing development and learning opportunities to nurture talent. This can include training programs, mentoring, coaching, and job rotations to broaden skills and enhance capabilities.

4. Performance Management and Feedback: Establish effective performance management systems that provide regular feedback, set clear expectations, and recognize achievements. This enables continuous improvement and growth.

5. Empowerment and Autonomy: Empower individuals by providing them with autonomy and decision-making authority within their roles. Encourage innovation and initiative, allowing individuals to contribute their unique perspectives and ideas.

6. Diversity and Inclusion: Foster a diverse and inclusive work environment that values different backgrounds, perspectives, and experiences. Embrace diversity as a catalyst for creativity, collaboration, and innovation.

7. Work-Life Integration: Promote work-life integration by encouraging work flexibility, promoting a healthy work-life balance, and providing support for personal well-being. This enhances employee satisfaction, engagement, and overall performance.

8. Recognition and Rewards: Implement a comprehensive recognition and rewards program that acknowledges and appreciates the contributions of high-performing individuals and teams. This reinforces a culture of excellence and motivates continuous achievement.

The Journey Towards Success

The journey towards leveraging the power of talent in operations is not without its challenges. It requires commitment, perseverance, and a willingness to adapt. Here are some key principles to guide organizations on this journey:

1. Adaptability: Embrace change and be adaptable in the face of evolving market dynamics and technological advancements. Embrace new ways of working and encourage a growth mindset.

2. Collaboration: Foster collaboration within and across teams, departments, and functions. Encourage open

Chapter 12: The Power of Talent in Operations: A Journey of Success

communication, knowledge sharing, and cross-functional problem-solving to drive collective success.

3. Data-Driven Decision Making: Utilize data and analytics to make informed decisions. Leverage data to identify patterns, uncover insights, and drive continuous improvement.

4. Innovation and Continuous Improvement: Encourage a culture of innovation and continuous improvement. Embrace new ideas, experimentation, and creative problem-solving to stay ahead of the competition.

5. Agility: Cultivate organizational agility to respond quickly and effectively to changing

market demands. Foster a culture that embraces flexibility, adaptability, and resilience.

6. Learning Organization: Strive to become a learning organization that values and invests in employee development. Encourage a thirst for knowledge, support continuous learning, and create avenues for sharing best practices.

7. Leadership Excellence: Develop exceptional leaders who can inspire, motivate, and guide their teams to

achieve exceptional results. Invest in leadership development programs and provide opportunities for leaders to grow and evolve.

By embracing these principles and nurturing a culture of talent excellence, organizations can embark on a transformative journey towards operational success. The power of talent becomes a driving force that propels the organization forward, fostering innovation, driving efficiency, and ultimately delivering superior value to customers.

Conclusion: Unleashing the Power of Talent in Operations

As we bring our exploration to a close, it is evident that talent is the cornerstone of operational success. Organizations that invest in recruiting, developing, and empowering a skilled workforce are poised to achieve remarkable results. High-performing teams, exceptional managers, a culture of continuous improvement, and a focus on maintaining momentum all contribute to unleashing the power of talent in operations.

However, this journey is not static. It requires continuous effort, adaptability, and a commitment to nurturing talent. By embracing a holistic approach to talent management, organizations can create an environment where individuals thrive, innovation flourishes, and operational excellence becomes the norm.

As leaders and managers, it is our responsibility to champion the power of talent, to foster a culture that supports growth and development, and to harness the collective abilities of our teams. By doing so, we can unlock the full potential of talent in operations and pave the way for enduring success.

Let us embrace this journey with enthusiasm and dedication, for the power of talent knows no bounds when unleashed in the realm of operations. Together, we can create a future where organizations thrive, individuals excel, and the transformative impact of talent resonates far and wide.

www.ingramcontent.com/pod-product-compliance
Lightning Source LLC
Chambersburg PA
CBHW070126230526
45472CB00004B/1447